MW00942514

The 25 Days of Christmas Cocktailing

One Man. One Month. One Very Merry Mission.

By Dino Tripodis

To all of the more-than-patient women,
who tolerate their less-than-sensible men.

And to my mother, who said nothing
good would come of my drinking.

Table of Contents

How The Whole, Crazy Thing Got Started

I'm a giver. Ask anyone. On Monday nights for the past 15 years, there's been a standing poker game at my house with most of the original players still representing the bulk of the table. I supply the booze, the food, the cards, the chips, various snacks and a fine musical selection of over 1000 albums (that's right...albums) which play magnificently on a huge brown Fisher stereo that came out of someone's living room and made its way into my basement. The generosity doesn't stop there. I tend to lose more than I win on most Mondays, but like I said- I'm a giver.

Cocktails play a large part in Monday Night Poker. A few of them are poured before the game as the players trickle in and then more make their way into the basement once the cards are "in the air."

"Cocktails" have always played a large part in our social circle. When the holidays roll around that circle becomes a festive wreath of camaraderie. Maybe it's the "joy of the season," but during the holidays, we seem to find additional reasons and opportunities to get together more often to toast our friendships, alleviate our stress, and test our vital organs.

The exact year escapes me, but I think it was December of 2004, I got the idea to embark on a journey I simply named, *The 25 Days of Christmas Cocktailing*. The goal was simple. I would attempt to have a different kind of drink from December 1st right on through to the 25th. Mind you, it wasn't about 25 days of drunken stupors. Instead, it would be more of a festive sampling of other libations that were not part of my normal drinking patterns.

As I mentioned- I'm a giver, and a confirmed Jack Daniel's drinker. The 25 Days would be my way of "giving back" by paying attention to some of the other liquors I unintentionally ignored 11 months of the year. Bring on the rums, gins, vodkas, scotches, beers, and wines of the world! All would be equal in my eyes during the month of December.

What started as a lark of an idea quickly became a tradition. Bartenders at my favorite local establishments anticipated the approaching holiday and the consistency of my patronage. Through the years, a handful of hearty and adventurous friends would attempt the mission with me. Most failed. Some came close to completing all 25 days, but ultimately they just...could not...make it. It was a spirited call to say the least. It required commitment, adversity and a decent amount of cash. It was not a mission for the weak, the timid, or anyone with "gout." It was time consuming, vocationally damaging and at times- relationship straining. But it was also Christmas, dammit, and deep in my heart, liver and kidneys I felt that "tis the season" needed some real significance again.

As is the case with most traditions, the official honoring of one can unintentionally become routine and casually expected. In 2008, after a hearty Thanksgiving, I asked myself what I could do to inject some new enthusiasm to the cause. And then it hit me. I would create my own holiday cocktails with their own unique and festive names.

I would embark upon a ridiculous journey of creativity and originality that would elevate The 25 Days of Christmas Cocktailing to splendid new heights! However, I couldn't do it alone. Santa had elves to assist him. I would have to recruit some elves of my own.

The Cocktail Coalition

On Christmas Day, three wise men traveled afar to witness the birth of the baby Jesus. I needed three not-so-wise men to witness the creation of the 25 different cocktails I was about to bestow on the world. Then of course, I needed them to taste the concoctions to see if they were worthy of consumption. The two events do not even begin to parallel one another. For starters, I was making these drinks in a house, not a manger and while trying to make cocktails with various livestock lying around sounds like a good time, it really tends to complicate the process.

Chris Delafeld, Chris Beardman, and Jamie Sanfillipo were the chosen ones. They had the time, the initiative, and very understanding wives. They were also part of another Christmas tradition I had started a few years back- Christmas Dropping, which is simply a strategic day and night of holiday shopping and drinking. I'll be honest. There's usually more drinking than shopping on this annual outing and the outcome is usually the purchasing of gifts that our significant others stare at politely with disappointment in their eyes and not-so-hidden contempt in their hearts. Half the time, what we bought was wrapped on the spot at the store we purchased it from and we didn't even remember what our lovelies were opening. However, one would think that crystal reindeer from the Swarovski shop and thongs and teddies from Victoria's Secret would bring joy to any woman on Christmas Day. Ignorance is bliss. During the holidays, it's apparently the loyal and hearty companion of stupidity.

The first seven days of invention were fun and full of laughter, embracing the novelty of the idea and toasting to our successes. The next ten days however, felt like work; having to arrive at a certain time each day, adjusting schedules, fighting seasonal colds and sometimes frustrated wives who initially thought the idea was "cute" but never believed we'd see the mission to its drunken completion..

The last eight days were full of determination, dedication, and an unanticipated condition I aptly termed as "liquor fatigue." Ah, but when The 25 Days Of Christmas Cocktailing came to a close, there was no escaping the sense of accomplishment we all felt; no denial of the pride that swelled our chests and no complaints of the ache that pinched our livers. The only question that remains is- are YOU up for the challenge? Can you become an honorary member of The Cocktail Coalition? A festive journey awaits you, my friends, as do a handful of headaches, a couple of hangovers, and maybe a sick day or two. On the other hand, it does give a completely new meaning to the "spirit of the season." Merry Christmas and Happy Holidays!

A Disclaimer About The Author

I am not a professional mixologist. I had a brief stint as a bartender in Wheeling, W.Va. when I was 19 years old at a fine establishment known as The Office Lounge. The gig lasted about a month and a half. It only lasted that long because the drink requests were simple ones. Once people started asking for cocktails that involved more than whiskey, rum, vodka or gin and a mixer, my reply of, "no, how about something else" ran its short but enjoyable course.

However, in my home I have no less than three fully stocked bars- well four if you count the little one in my office...scratch that- five (I forgot the little fold away bar in the bedroom). Okay, I have five bars in my home and two additional refrigerators solely dedicated to water, sodas, and beer. So, in some respect I do feel qualified to have written this book and now realize I may not be normal. Also, note that I did a lot of research in the creating of these cocktails, trying to infuse some originality in my attempt to bring something fresh and new to the drunken table. Keeping that in mind, THERE ARE A LOT OF DRINKS OUT THERE! Therefore, if one of my Christmas Cocktails goes by a Brazilian Wax Job in South America or The Queen's Candy Cane in England, or A Presidential Pardon in Texas, I apologize, and with all due respect- get over it. I did not embark on this project to change the drinking world. I only wanted to make it a more festive place to imbibe in. Enjoy.

What You Are Going To Need

If it is your sincere desire to make ALL of these cocktails, well GOOD LUCK and GOD BLESS! You will need the following ingredients. These are NOT available at your favorite liquor store, but instead must come from you, the brave and festive drinker.

(2) FUNCTIONING KIDNEYS
(1) RELATIVELY UNSCARRED LIVER
(1) VERY UNDERSTANDING SIGNIFICANT OTHER
(1) DECENT LAWYER ON RETAINER (OPTIONAL)
(1) BOTTLE OF IBUPROFEN

The Necessary Bottles of Booze and Mixers

Jack Daniels

Bailey's

Bacardi Gold Rum

Extra Dry Vermouth

Myers's Dark Rum

Disaronno

Maker's Mark Whiskey

Absolute Vodka

Cherry Schnappes

Old Overhold Rye Whiskey

Gin

Crème de Menthe

Brandy

Peppermint Schnappes

Cinnamon Schnappes

Patron Silver Tequila

Dewars Scotch

Black Sambuca

Clear (White) Sambuca

Bass Ale

Crown Royal

Goldshlagger

Caramel Crème Liquer

Banana Luquer

Chambord

Grand Marnier

Carlo Rossi Paisano Wine

Chocolate Liquer

Drambuie

Peach Schnappes

Jameson's Whiskey

Bacardi Silver Rum

Malibu Rum

Ouzo

Black Tea

Cranberry Juice

7-Up

Orange Juice

Honey

Instant Espresso

Lime Juice

Grenadine

Ginger Ale

Triple Sec

Coffee

Cherry 7-Up

Soda Water

Lots of Ice

*Stupidity

* This ingredient is optional, but may help in your journey.

Day 1 **The Jack Frost**

1 SHOT OF JACK DANIEL'S
1 SHOT OF BAILEY'S
1 TEASPOON OF INSTANT ESPRESSO
1 DASH OF TRIPLE SEC

Shake with ice and pour into a tall glass, then top it off with club soda.

"Jack Daniel's can make for a mean drunk.
Frank Sinatra drank Jack Daniel's.
Therefore, Peter Lawford got his ass kicked a lot!"

~Dino Tripodis 1998

Jack-Be-Not-So-Nimble

You should know that for years I was a confirmed single malt scotch drinker. Glenlivet was my choice for every day drinking and on occasion I would taste and experiment with other fine single malts in an attempt to broaden my scotch horizons.

I am also a huge Frank Sinatra fan. We (my friends and I) had a pact. When the sad day arrived that Frank Sinatra would pass, the plan was to drop whatever we were doing and meet at our favorite bar. At the time, it was a place called The Blue Danube in Columbus, Ohio. Upon arrival, the only drink allowed would be Jack Daniel's- Franks' favorite, and the green label Jack if you want to get technical. He died on Thursday, May 14, 1998. We received the news the following morning. He had died the night before, but well...we were drinking and missed it. By 11:00 a.m. that Friday morning, we were all in place and a toasting tribute that we have yet to match concluded sometime around 11:00 p.m. Saturday night. Frank would have been proud. The torch and spirit of The Rat Pack had been passed on and I'm sure we spilled it on more than one occasion. I've been a devout Jack Daniel's man ever since. So, "here's one for my baby, and one more for the road." Oh, and I apologize to everyone I spoke to during that "tribute." I had no business answering the phone.

Day 2 The Rum Rum Rudolph

1 SHOT OF BACARDI GOLD
1 SHOT OF MALIBU RUM
1 SHOT OF MAKERS MARK
DASH OF GRENADINE

Shake with ice, pour into tall glass and mix with equal parts
7-Up and orange juice, and add a touch of grenadine.
Do not let the recipient of this drink guide anyone's sleigh.

*"The difference between social drinking and binge drinking is mathematical,
with the correct answer being nine."*

~Dino Tripodis 2000

Ho-Ho-Ho, And A Bottle Of Rum

When I think of rum, I think of pirates. When I think of pirates, I think of Johnny Depp. When I think of Johnny Depp, I ask myself "why" and "am I gay?" Then I think of one of my favorite Johnny Depp movies, DONNIE BRASCO and realize, I'm not gay, and it's not really about Johnny Depp. I'm just a huge Al Pacino fan. Then I put on some holiday music from Chuck Berry and make this.

Day 3 A Very Merry Vodka

2 SHOTS OF ABSOLUTE VODKA
2 SHOTS OF CHERRY SCHNAPPES
CHERRY 7-UP
TOUCH OF GRENADINE

Shake the vodka and schnapps with ice, and pour into a tall glass. Top it off with Cherry 7-UP and cap it off with a touch of Grenadine.

"Never drink vodka with a Russian. Even when you're boozin', there's such a thing as "home field advantage."

~Dino Tripodis 2002

Shaken? Stirred? Who Cares? Just Serve!

If you are going to entertain, then vodka is a "must have" in your liquor arsenal. It's a requirement for most martinis; which we will concoct later in the book, and most importantly- women love vodka! In addition, the more flavors you have on hand, the better. I know this from experience. While hosting a party a woman asked if I had any orange vodka. When I said "no" she looked at me with disappointment and disdain as though I had just farted. She wasn't an invited guest and left with whomever she came with, but since then I have tried to stock some additional flavors at the bar. If you can make half the drinks consumed on HBO's *Sex & The City*, then consider yourself more than equipped for a night of home entertaining.

With women, vodkas are like shoes: the more you have to choose from, in both color and style, the better your chances of making a sale- assuming of course that you are actually trying to close one.

This vodka creation can be enjoyed as a cocktail over ice or can kick off an evening of seasonal shooters. If you would like to attach a challenge to this drink, try saying "very, merry vodka" three times fast, after just two of these. I'm still trying.

Day 4 You're A Mean Drunk, Mr. Grinch

OLD OVERHOLT RYE WHISKEY

Pour it over ice and leave them alone.

"There's no bad place to sleep when you're drunk."

~Dino Tripodis 2007

A Crotchety-Tail

There is no escaping a Grinch at Christmas. It's that person who gripes and moans about the holiday as soon as the Halloween candy goes on sale, and the way-too-early Christmas displays go up. The person who hates Christmas music played before Thanksgiving, and the person who probably was told there's no such thing as Santa at 6 years of age. Wait a minute- that's me.

Okay, maybe a lot of us share those sentiments, but once the season is in full swing, I am IN, baby! The real Grinch is the person- who once the season is officially underway- you'll find sitting at the end of the bar; nursing their drink, mumbling to themselves about the ridiculous cost of the holiday, and how much they hate mall choirs, over-priced Christmas trees, holiday kiosks with toy helicopters flying everywhere, and Santa Land displays. They'll grouse on how there are too many Christmas specials on television, arena shows "on ice" and in a brief moment of holiday sentiment, will bemoan the fact that Andy Williams hasn't come out with a new Christmas album in almost 40 years. But enough about my father.

So, if there is a Grinch in your holiday plans, serve up this simple beverage and ask them to refrain from throwing up in the poinsettia.

Day 5 Gin-Gle Bells

1 OUNCE OF GIN
1 OUNCE OF VODKA
1 1/2 OUNCE OF CRÈME DE MENTHE
GINGER ALE

Shake with ice and strain into a rocks glass filling it 3/4 full, top the rest of the shot off with ginger ale.

"The only difference between getting drunk with your mom as opposed to your dad is you feel worse about the fist fight afterwards."

~Dino Tripodis 1996

Christmas Bells Are Drinking

Seriously. Does anyone drink gin anymore? Yes! My mother, (God bless her). Nothing warms the heart more during the holidays than having mom belly up to your bar and say "Gin me, son." Seeing her all decked out with some abomination of a Christmas sweater, you pour a little heavy because you know memories to last a lifetime are fast approaching.

After one, she gets a little flush with color. After two she gets a little giggly, but not so much that she can't tell you to set her up again before that second one is empty. If you're lucky, by the third one she might tell you how she almost slept with Jerry Lewis when he and Dean Martin worked the Capitol Theater in Steubenville, Ohio, but couldn't go through with it because Jerry kept yelling "Hey laaaady!"

Okay, maybe I'm making some of this up, and then again, maybe I'm not. My point is this: gin is an "old school" drink, and you should show some respect for the boozing veteran that asks for it. Moreover, it's a charming little liquor and who knows- after mixing up this lovely holiday shooter, you just might get your mom talking, too.

Day 6 The George Bailey

1 CUP OF COFFEE
1 SHOT OF BAILEYS
1/2 SHOT OF BRANDY
1/2 SHOT OF BACARDI RUM
1/2 SHOT OF MAKERS MARK WHISKEY
A DASH OF TRIPLE SEC

Stir quietly and ask if there is pie.

"I don't drink compulsively. I drink consistently. There's a difference."

~Dino Tripodis 2004

You'll Wish You Had Never Been Born

Our first coffee drink. Who doesn't like a good, steaming cup of Joe during the holidays? Especially when it has enough liquor in it to make you run down the wintry streets of your hometown yelling, "It IS a wonderful life!"

The movie, by the way, is my all-time favorite during the holidays, but credit for the name of the drink has to go to my old college roommate, who I think peed a little with excitement when he found out he would be part of such a magnificent literary undertaking.

Makes you put the film's message into perspective, does it not? Imagine if my roommate had never been born. The name for this drink may have never come to fruition. We never would've been roommates at THE Ohio State University. I wouldn't be Godfather to his only son. He wouldn't be 51 years of age and constantly asking himself, "what went wrong in my life?" And I wouldn't be there to reassure him with soothing explanations like "you just made some bad choices...starting with your roommate in college."

Enjoy The George Bailey as you reflect on your own life and times. And if they're bad...have a second cup.

Day 7 The Christmas Kamikaze

1 SHOT OF VODKA
1 SHOT OF RUM
1 SHOT OF GIN
1 SHOT OF PEPPERMINT SCHNAPPES
1 SHOT OF CINNAMON SCHNAPPES
1/3 CUP OF ORANGE JUICE
1/3 CUP OF CRANBERRY JUICE
ONE SOLID POUR OF TRIPLE SEC

Make it, shake it, and pour it into a really tall glass that takes a long time to finish.

"I remember when the "designated driver" was the one friend who could find the car."

~Dino Tripodis 2006

Crashin' Into Christmas

A seasonal twist on an old favorite, the Christmas kamikaze, was one of the holiday drinks that made me take away the car keys from The Cocktail Coalition during its "sample phase." The taste of the drink is extremely pleasant and goes down way too smoothly, but its power is an unsuspecting one and can most definitely lead to a crash and burn scenario.

If you have holiday revelers on a "mission", this cocktail mix will more assuredly help get them there. However, I cannot stress this enough: no matter what your friend's "mission," be it a good time, or an attempt to forget a bad time, you want everyone in your platoon back safe to do battle again tomorrow. Because (start stirring theme music here), Rome wasn't built in a day, and it's not what you know, it's who you know, and more importantly- who knows what you know because that person could be trouble later in life. And a bird in the hand is...well...it's weird if you're not a magician, and if you're not part of the solution, then you're just part of the problem- unless of course you never asked to be part of the solution, which then technically should no longer make it your problem. Am I right?! But let's be honest- people make assumptions all the time and that, my friends, that is why the divorce rate in this country is still at almost 50%! Mmm... did I mention that these drinks go down rather smoothly?

Over The River, Through The Woods, And Under Some Unexpected Pressure

If you made it through the first seven days- congratulations, you have done some fine work. You're probably having fun and maybe have even started your own "cocktail coalition." (T-shirts are available) I hope that you and your friends have gotten together and bonded over cocktails and conversation, which was always one of the primary goals.

Our first week was a blast as well, and in many ways wasn't that much different from a typical week of socializing; lots of stories and laughs mixed in with some holiday venting and if time wasn't an issue- a little bit of food.

Ah, yes. The first week was fun, frivolous, and fascinating from an alcohol perspective. We all agreed that this was going to be the best month ever! But one week does not a month make.

As we entered into our second week of Christmas Cocktailing, schedules became an issue. Some members of the Coalition were late on occasion and as I may have mentioned earlier, some wives quickly tired of hearing, "I'm at Dino's trying the latest cocktail." Not to mention the pressure I had unknowingly put on myself.

I was coming home everyday after working a morning radio shift at Sunny 95. My day started at 4:00 a.m. I was arriving home at approximately 11:00 a.m. and going right into the bar, which I had affectionately renamed, "The Cocktail Kitchen." Armed with no more than a name for the cocktail and a liquor-filled imagination, I would go to work trying to find the right blends and mixes, taste testing all of my the mistakes and by 1:00 p.m. would be "half-in-the-bag" in the name of Libationary Science. I know that's not a real science, but neither was Scientology until L. Ron Hubbard invented it and look how many people devote their lives to that "invention". By the way, if you are a Scientologist, I'm not judging. I think you deserve a cocktail as much as anyone else after a hard day of spiritual cleansing.

The standing appointment for the Coalition was daily at 3:00 p.m. Some would get there at four and we would try to wrap things up by five, with the emphasis on "tried ." It's one thing to come home from work and crack open a beer, or pour your favorite scotch into a glass of rocks. It is an entirely different set of endeavors to come home from work, invent a drink, seek approval for the cocktail you have created, then debate with your significant other why what you've deemed "a holiday mission" is more important than meeting her and her sister for dinner.

It was proving to be a challenge for me on the creating side and just as much of a challenge for the coalition on the consuming side. Nevertheless, there was no turning back now. The very, merry mission continued.

Day 8 The Ebeneezer Scrooge-Driver

1 1/2 SHOT OF VODKA
1 SHOT OF PATRON SILVER TEQUILA
1 SHOT OF BACARDI GOLD
A DASH OF ROSE'S GRENADINE
A DASH OF ROSE'S LIME JUICE
AND OF COURSE, ORANGE JUICE

Place all the liquors into a shaker with ice and mix. Pour it into a tall glass and top it off with the orange juice. If you're into garnishes, a lovely cherry will top this cocktail off nicely before you drink a few of these and wake up afraid that you've missed Christmas.

"What's my definition of a Tequila Sunrise?
Waking up by noon after a bottle of Patron the night before."

~Dino Tripodis 1991

A Visit By No Less Than Three Spirits

This one was tricky for me because there was Tequila in the mix, and Tequila and I- let's just say we don't get along anymore. At first, I was going to ignore that particular liquor, but then one night the Ghosts of Drunken Stupors Past, Present, and Future paid me a visit and took me on a journey that taught me to face my liquor fears rather than ignore them.

The first spirit who looked a lot like my Aunt Nicky, took me back to my senior year of high school in Steubenville. We had crossed the bridge into West Virginia with fake I.D.'s and were ready to be grown-ups.

It was my first experience with tequila and the Spirit quickly took me to the ultimate outcome- me, hugging the toilet bowl in a Frisch's Big Boy restaurant. From there we were quickly whisked to a place in my stand-up comedy past where I found myself face down on the floor of my apartment with no shirt, no pants and no recollection of how I had gotten there.

"I get it, spirit," I said. "I shouldn't drink tequila."

"Is that what you really think the lesson is?" asked my Aunt Nicky and then laughed maniacally as she disappeared to make room for my next visit.

The second spirit, who looked like Frank Sinatra, took me to the recent present. It was a Cinco de Mayo celebration where I stood in the background like a Mormon, apparently afraid to even get close to the scent of anything that might've rhymed with Patron.

"What?" I said. "I'm behaving myself. I'm staying away from tequila."

"Yeah, you are. And you're the life of the party," Frank said with no lack of sarcasm. "It's a pity, is all. A pity. But go ahead, and keep nursin' that beer, kid."

Frank left and knowing how the story goes, I waited for that ominous, silent, third spirit- well, ominous if you consider it was my friend Mikey, draped in a cape from a Darth Vader costume he never took back. He took to me an unmarked grave in Mexico and just pointed.

"Is this my future?" I asked. "I die drinking tequila in Mexico and then I'm buried in some unmarked grave? Say, it isn't so, spirit! Say, it isn't so."

"Actually," said Mikey. "It's not. I did that for effect. The truth of the matter is after facing your fear of tequila in the book, you go on to invent a tequila "energy" drink, which makes you millions. The only reason we're in Mexico is because you have a summer home down here and I'm living in it."

The lesson? People don't really change, but they can drink tequila again.

Day 9 The Scotch Pine Spritzer

1 SHOT OF DEWARS BLENDED SCOTCH
1 SHOT OF GIN
1 SHOT CRÈME DE MENTHE
1 DASH OF TRIPLE SEC

Mix all of the above ingredients in a shaker with ice, pour into
a tall glass, and top it off with some ginger ale.

"If an idea sounds debatable when you're sober, but then great when you're
drinking, it will have become a bad idea by morning."

~Dino Tripodis 2005

If A Drunk Falls In The Forest...

I guess there are some people that still like to get their Christmas tree the old-fashioned way. They like to get into a car with friends or family and ride out to some Christmas tree farm where the freshly fallen snow makes for a picturesque setting that Norman Rockwell himself would've painted.

Unless of course you are my friends. If that's the case, you're still going out to that farm with the best intentions of getting the perfect tree, but are probably "half-in-the-bag" by the time you get there and more than likely never bothered to ask if anyone in the group is actually skilled with an axe. So, after finding that perfect specimen of holiday splendor you proceed to "cut 'er down" but never get to finish because that slight "slip" of the axe just cut deep into your friend's leg and now you're finding that the "perfect tree" is not so much the concern as is keeping your friend from bleeding out. One of the idiots suggests wrapping the wound with duct tape, but then someone else in the group thinks they know how to make a tourniquet with your girlfriend's scarf. Meanwhile, your bleeding friend is close to lapsing into unconsciousness as you drive like hell back into town, the whole time yelling, "Hold on, man! We're almost there. We're almost there!"

Then, after getting your friend to the emergency room in time to save the leg, you breathe a sigh of relief and take comfort in the fact that another holiday tragedy has been averted. That's when you all gather around a nice fire, recap the day's events, promise your girlfriend you'll replace the bloodied scarf, and question whether or not your friend will have a noticeable limp. Happy Holidays, indeed.

Day 10 **The Lump Of Coal**

Get a rocks glass. Fill it with ice. Pour Black Sambuca over the ice and watch the thickness of the liquor blanket those ice cubes like a black sweater that goes with everything; be it your mood, temperament, or the Currier and Ives Christmas socks you received early from your aunt in Pittsburgh.

"Simple drinks are like bad relationships. They both wind up on the rocks, but at least the drinks end with a cheaper tab."

~Dino Tripodis 1999

A Diamond In The Stuff

Normally during Christmas, a lump of coal is associated with bad behavior, punishment for not being a good boy or girl. Needless to say, I've gotten a lot of coal through the years.

However, for our holiday cocktail purposes, I thought Day 10 needed another shot of simplicity in the mix and so THE LUMP OF COAL was created. As you'll see in the ingredients portion, the cleverness and ingenuity is all in the name, a festive moniker to describe a simple pour of booze into ice, and sometimes- aren't the simplest things the ones we appreciate most during Christmas?

The truth of the matter is, I was in a time crunch that day as was the Coalition, but we could not risk falling behind. "Catching up" in the creation of these cocktails was not an option. I did not want the making of these drinks to be like "last-minute" Christmas shopping.

We've all been there. A panic sinks in during those last few frantic hours on Christmas Eve when you realize the only store open is a Sunoco gas station, so you convince yourself that a metal die-cast gas truck has to be good for someone on your list. You buffer that with some holiday scratch off lottery tickets, a carton of smokes and festive 12-pack of Heineken, and you walk out of that Sunoco feeling a little better about yourself and the holiday. Forget the fact that your proud purchases are best suited for a recent parolee, or a creepy uncle you only see once a year. However, if you're shopping for my family...that usually can knock two people off the list.

Day 11 O, Tan And Bombed

1 PINT OF HARPS OR BASS (The Tan)
1 SHOT OF CROWN (The Bombed)
1 SHOT OF BRANDY
1 AND 1⁄2 SHOTS OF CARAMEL CREAM LIQUOR

Throw all parts into a shaker with ice, mix, and strain into a shot glass. The two tastes (the beer and the shot) will get along better than your parents.

"I have no desire to drink anyone under the table.
It's crowded down there and the service sucks!"

~Dino Tripodis 2008

A Not-So-Odd Couple

The beer and a shot drinker. The simple consumer of alcohol. They don't need much. Just an icy, cold beer and a shot of familiarity to go along with it. They have no desire for fancy drinks that take longer to make than they do to order. They just want that less-than-dynamic duo served up quickly with a minimum of conversation in the process.

That's been me on many an occasion. A desire to cut to the chase and get on with it. If there's going to be conversation then let me start it, bartender. Don't ask me "how I'm doin'." I just ordered a beer and a shot. How do you think I'm doing? I probably laid cash on the bar and didn't pick it up when you gave me my change, so, yeah- I'm not going anywhere anytime soon. Check on me frequently because the shots-to-beer ratio is tricky and different with each individual drinker and this particular round of boozin' will be about balance.

I'm sure we'll engage in conversation eventually and the subject matter will be things you're already acquainted with, so just nod and agree with me because I'm probably not in the mood for debate.

Maybe our conversation will be about women. Or, maybe it'll be about work. Or, maybe it'll be about women at work. Or, why men and women emotionally don't work. Or, why does it take so much damn work to find a good woman? Or, "I wish, I didn't have to work." Ah, but if you don't work, you don't get paid. If you don't get paid, you can't go out. If you can't go out, you won't meet anybody, and if you don't meet anybody how are you ever going to regain the false hope that maybe, just maybe you have found your soul mate at a place called "BOB'S."

Even the beer and a shot drinker needs a little bit of Christmas cheer. So, if you find yourself on that familiar stool in that familiar bar and want to bring a little joy to the season, try this festive little combination I've created. Note that even though it's the simplicity of a beer and a shot, I took it a step further to ensure that the two tastes compliment one another in a lovely seasonal way. Just because you can't get along with anybody doesn't mean your liquor has to follow suit.

Day 12 **Yellow Snow**

2 SHOTS OF BANANA LIQUOR
1 SHOT OF BACARDI LIGHT RUM
1 SHOT OF BACARDI GOLD RUM
2 SHOTS OF ORANGE JUICE
1 SHOT OF TRIPLE SEC

Put all of the ingredients, with ice, into the blender and mix to a frothy white glass of fun. Once properly blended there should also be a tinge of yellow (from the o.j.) giving it that holiday glow. And please...do not try to write your name in it.

"Peeing when you're drunk is like shooting a gun for the first time. Your aim might be off, but you're thrilled you at least hit the target."

~Dino Tripodis 2003

Snow-Flaky

"And don't you eat that yellow snow." However, you can drink it! By the 12th Day of Christmas Cocktailing, I was feeling a bit artistic and avant-garde. A poker associate gave the potential name for the cocktail to me, and as soon as he said it, I knew I had to make it. I say "poker associate" because that sounds better than degenerate card player friend.

Anyway, the thought of creating something delicious that initially sounds vile and disgusting was very appealing to me. To be able to create a cocktail based on the idiocy of relieving yourself in a snowdrift captivated my imagination and urinary tract, but I also knew that this was going to be one of those cocktails that would have to "look the part" as well. As a result- our first blender drink. It's festive. It's fun. In addition, it's a conversation starter.

"What are you drinking?"

"Yellow Snow."

"Eww. That sounds disgusting. Can I try it?"

"Mmmm. That's delicious. Where can I get some Yellow Snow?"

At this point, if the person you are talking to takes you anywhere other than back to the bar, walk away. He has a different agenda and more than likely has crashed the party.

13 Drinks And Me, The Only Bar In Town

Don't think it didn't come up. "Why can't you just be happy with 12 days of Christmas Cocktailing?" Well, if I had started that way years ago when I was just drinking a different cocktail everyday and had chosen to follow along with the traditional 12 days, then maybe the following words could've been part of a lovely epilog. However, that's not the case. 25 was the number selected, so 25 would be the number of cocktails made. I'm stubborn in that regard. And determined. And stupid. Ask my girlfriend. Especially regarding the stupid part.

The Cocktail Coalition was still showing up on a daily basis, but I could detect that they, too were wondering if this endeavor would wind up on the woodpile of great ideas that would never come to fruition. I sensed a lack of faith. I could see it in their blood-shot eyes, that look of "we ain't gonna make it, are we?"

"It's too much," said Deli. "Nobody really expects you to finish."

"I'll admit," said Beardman. "It's harder than I thought it would be."

"My wife hates me," said Jamie.

I'll admit it. I was having my fair share of doubts as well. Then all those wonderful clichés came pouring into my liquor-soused brain. "Rome wasn't built in a day." "You miss 100% of the shots you don't take." "Don't play cards with an alcoholic nun named, Sam."

Then all of the great inventions that changed the drinking game forever came rushing into my head like a flood of determination: the liquor pourer, the screw top cap, and the Taco Bell late-night-drive-thru window. I couldn't give up now! I couldn't stop in the middle of a dream only to let it become a nightmare of unrealized potential.

"I'm not stopping," I said. "Are you guys still with me?"

"All we gotta do is drink. You're the one makin' the cocktails. Do you think you can do it?" asked Deli.

"Jack Daniel as my witness, I'm certainly going to try," I replied.

"It's hard, but I'm no quitter," said Beardman.

"How much can one woman hate," said Jamie. "I'm in."

"Then, 'cheers' gentlemen," I said with a raised glass and false hope. "I'll see you all back here tomorrow." Nobody moved. "Or you can just stay. That's good too." And the very, merry mission stumbled onward.

Day 13 The Red Ryder B.B. Gun

1 SHOT OF BOURBON
1 SHOT OF BRANDY
1 SHOT OF CINNAMON SCHAPPES
A DASH OF GRENADINE

Pour all the shots into a shaker with ice and mix, then strain them into individual shot glasses.

"Drinking yourself "blind" is obviously temporary, because in the morning you can still see what an ass you made of yourself the night before."

~Dino Tripodis 2008

An I For An I

"No, Ralphie. You'll shoot your eye out." One of the greatest lines from one of the greatest holiday movies ever, *A Christmas Story*. Therefore, it goes without saying that the Red Ryder B.B. Gun would have to be a shot drink. Moreover, much like a pellet gun, the shot needed to have some substance to it, but at the same time not inflict any real harm.

As I began mixing up various combinations of liquors to make The Red Ryder shot, I found myself thinking back and wondering if at any time in our drinking history, had we actually "put an eye out." Yes. Yes, we have. And that's all you really need to know. Let's move on, shall we?

Day 14 We Three Kings Disoriented Are

1 SHOT OF CROWN ROYAL
1 SHOT OF CHAMBORD
1 SHOT OF GRAND MARNIER
1 DASH OF GRENADINE

Pour them all into a shaker with ice and mix thoroughly, and then strain the royal concoction into a shot glass.

OPTION: You can also pour this mix over ice and top it off with 7-UP and turn it into a powerful cocktail, which then makes it a "WE THREE KINGS DISORIENTED ARE BUT DON'T WANT TO PASS OUT AN HOUR INTO THE PARTY."

"I can usually remember the first drink of the night. It's the last one I need a little help with recollecting the following morning."

~Dino Tripodis 2007

"King, Me!"

"We Three Kings, disoriented are. Bearing booze we travel afar" You know how the song goes.

I wanted to go royal for this drink. I wanted the assortment of liquors to be majestic in their combination. Therefore, like a knight on a crusade I set out to find three libations that would be both noble and worthy of the cocktail about to be created. A King's Cocktail if you will, that once consumed would make you feel like you were drinking something of power and at the same time could reduce oneself to the silliness of a court jester.

I knew Crown Royal would be in the mix. That was an easy pick. The seal spoke to me, saying, "Pick me," and when liquor talks; I usually listen.

Then I came across a bottle of Chambord. The only reason I picked this one is that it had a crown for a bottle cap. Silly, I know, but once again let me remind you of the disclaimer in the beginning of this mess- I am not a professional mixologist. Just a drunk with a dream.

I could've stopped there, but the name of the drink is We Three Kings, so I felt the cocktail needed a third participant. Since I couldn't find anything else that had a crown related to it (or that didn't completely taste like crap when mixed with the other two liquors) I went grand and selected Grand Marnier as the third liquor. Disoriented yet? Oh, you will be.

Put this cocktail in the "taking one for the team" category. I must've gone through at least nine different combinations before coming up with that third magical bottle. By the time the Cocktail Coalition arrived to try it, I was a holiday mess, and I am not sure, but I might've been smoking some frankincense...and maybe some myrrh..., which is like smoking clove cigarettes, which by the way are nasty and DO NOT make you hipper than anyone else in the room. It just makes it easier for us to pick out the pretentious ass. Okay then...follow yonder star and enjoy.

Day 15 The Little Altar Boy

1 CUP OF CARLO ROSSI PAISANO WINE
1 SHOT OF GIN
1 SHOT OF VODKA
1/2 CUP OF 7-UP

Mix the wine, gin, and vodka in a shaker with ice and pour into a tall glass. Top it off with 7-UP. If you really want to dress it up, put a little water cracker on top as a floater. Then recite two Hail Mary's and one Our Father as penance for making and (even worse) enjoying this particular beverage.

"Wine is good medicine for the heart, sweet comfort for the soul, and is extremely over-priced at most of your finer restaurants."

~Dino Tripodis 2008

A Good Pour Of Penance

On Andy Williams' *Merry Christmas* album, you can find the beautiful, hymnal-like song, "Little Altar Boy". It's a fine piece of vocal styling that at times is almost haunting in its holiday message. The cocktail I created that was inspired by the song? Eh, not so much. Nevertheless, I wanted to incorporate some cheap wine into the cocktail creation mix. It's good for punch bowls and holiday acquaintances you don't want to waste the good stuff on.

But here's how my brain works. When I think of cheap wine, the first thing that comes to mind is communion wine; that capped bottle of Gallo or Riunite that sits back in the sacristy of any church or priest's office. That image pulls the trigger on my vague memories of church, which then knocks down the childhood dominos that are my recollections of being an altar boy. And when that chapter of my life re-surfaces, I thank the good Lord that I have no horrible deep-seeded memories that required a psychologist or memory aggression therapist.

The priest I served under- let me re-phrase that. The priest I served mass under was not without lust in his heart, but I'm relieved to say it was focused on women.

Even at a young age, I marveled watching this guy work his religious mojo while staying remarkably devoted to his faith and work in the church. It was like viewing your own small town version of The Thorn Birds.

One time, Father-No-Name, caught us pilfering communion wine from the sacristy. As a punishment, he made us drink all of the wine (a gallon of it) which made us sick as dogs and consequently topped the list for our next round of confession: admitting to stealing, drinking, and then throwing up the Blood of Christ. Who knew that particular life experience would someday inspire a holiday cocktail. It's true...the Lord does work in mysterious ways.

So, here's to you Father-Whose-Name-I-Don't-Have-Permission-To-Use. You offered guidance, life lessons and served as a unique, though sometimes confusing role model. But, I mean that in a good way. Peace be with you.

Day 16 The Christmas Drop

1 SHOT OF JACK DANIEL'S
1 SHOT OF CHOCOLATE LIQUER
1 SHOT OF PEPPERMINT SCHNAPPES

Put them all into a shaker with ice and then strain into a shot glass. You should find the shot smooth and reminiscent of a mint patty.

"Don't drink and drive.
Otherwise, how you gonna smoke?"

~Dino Tripodis 2008

Drop While You Shop

Christmas Dropping. A holiday custom started in 2002 whereupon one combines drinking and Christmas shopping with no real hope of serious retail accomplishments.

I mentioned our annual Christmas Dropping earlier in the book and when The Cocktail Coalition had finally secured a date and time to embark on the yearly fiasco, I felt it was my duty to create a shot to salute the time- honored tradition, hence Cocktail #16, THE CHRISTMAS DROP.

In its early days, Christmas Dropping just included Deli and me. We would pick a date, a time, and then flip a coin to see who would drive to the mall or shopping area of choice. Only in the last year few years has the tradition expanded to include the entire Coalition and with that expansion, a rented limousine added to the mix to ensure our safety. But please note: the freedom of said rented vehicle will increase your consumption of alcohol and drastically affect the productivity of gift buying for loved ones. That being said, these are the steps necessary for a successful Christmas Dropping:

1. Meet at the house of choice an hour before the car arrives.
2. Drink. Add some nice holiday meats and cheeses if so inclined.
3. Once in the car, drink some more, but before doing so, inform the driver that while the rental for the night may only last between 4 to 6 hours, it will feel more like 12 and apologize to that person often.
4. Pick a location in advance, preferably a mall or shopping area that has an abundance of bars and restaurants in addition to fine shopping.
5. Once you arrive at your first location-BUY SOMETHING! This accomplishes two things: one, you will actually be able to scratch a name off your list, and two, when your significant other undoubtedly calls to check to see if you've actually done any shopping, you can answer in the affirmative.
6. Try to stay together. Separation from the pack causes delays, confusion, and irresponsible purchasing.
7. Keep your receipts. If you have done your Christmas Dropping correctly, you will have purchased many stupid things that in hindsight no one will like.
8. Return to base and have one last shot before the hired car takes you back to your own home to face ridicule, shame, and questions you will not have good answers for when asked.

Day 17 The Little Drambuie Boy

1 SHOT OF DRAMBUIE
1 SHOT OF CROWN ROYAL
1 SHOT OF BRANDY
GINGER ALE
TOUCH OF GRENADINE

Pour all the ingredients into a shaker with ice, mix and then pour into a tall glass. Cap it off with some ginger ale.

"If you think you are "the life of the party" I can almost guarantee there are others in attendances that are waiting patiently for you to socially die."

~Dino Tripodis 1999

Bang A Drunk

Yes, this cocktail is in honor of The Little Drummer Boy. Sort of. The sweet story of the little boy, who unlike The Three Wise Men had no gift for the newborn King except for the rum, pum, pum, pum of his little drum. Nice. And as a story, it works in a manger for the birth of the baby Jesus. But, at a holiday party, it's a stretch.

How many times have you told your guests that everyone is bringing something to the party and STILL there is that handful of freeloaders that walk in empty-handed. Or worse- they come with an already opened bag of DORITOS for you to "throw into the mix."

A lot of the time, they are the first to arrive and sometimes the last to leave. They put that first big dent in the three-layer dip, take a "fisherman's net" serving of shrimp and make a sandwich big enough to save half of it for the ride home. Then, in the middle of their grazing, they tell you to fix them their "usual" and remind you to pour a little heavy because, "hey, it's a party."

Why are they there? You know why. Some of them are relatives and a party is not the time to question what went awry in your family's genetic pool. However, what I usually find to be the case is this: They belong to and are with someone else that you actually DO enjoy having in your home and the only way to get that person there is to accept the package deal that is the "significant other." Meanwhile you put on a fake smile and wonder to yourself, "When was that low self-esteem day that this loser swept in and took advantage of my friend, and how have they managed to continue to pull it off?"

DO NOT make THIS drink for THAT guest. It's expensive and tasty and you don't want it to become his new "usual." Doritos, my ass...

Day 18 The Snow Globe

1 SHOT OF CLEAR SAMBUCA
1 SHOT OF BACARDI SILVER RUM
1 SHOT OF ABSOLUTE VODKA
7-UP

Mix the liquors in a shaker with ice and pour into a large rocks glass. Top it off with 7-up and because of the Sambuca, initially it should actually look like a snow globe settling down after a good shake. Yes, it's pretty, picturesque, and potent.

"On most trips what "happens in Vegas" is I lose, and what "stays in Vegas" is my money. But the drinks are free, so there's a win in there somewhere."

~Dino Tripodis 2009

A Snow "Job"

Ah, the snow globe. That lovely picturesque scene contained in a glass or plastic bubble, which is then picked up and violently shaken so you can blissfully watch the chaotic little particles of snow settle back down to their original point of serenity.

I have a couple of snow globes that I purchased in Las Vegas. One of them has little dice instead of snow and when you shake it always rolls craps or a seven after you've established the point.

Another one has little hands of black jack cards, that once they settle into place add up to something just over 21. I also have a little slot machine snow globe that never shakes into a winner.

If I could make my own Vegas snow globes, I assure you the scenes would be different. Look at this one. When you shake it, the snow is actually money from all my winnings falling around me. Oh and here's one of me in the upgraded penthouse suite they gave me after hitting a huge slot machine jackpot. All the little snow particles are comps. This one is probably the most realistic of the bunch. It's me back at home after a losing trip to Vegas. The little flakes of snow are all of the white lies about how much money I said I lost compared to the amount of money I actually came home with. Yes, a lot DOES stay in Vegas.

Day 19 Silver And Gold

1 SHOT OF BACARDI SILVER
1 SHOT OF GOLDSHLAGGER SCHNAPPES
1 DASH OF LIME JUICE

Toss them all into a shaker with ice, chill and pour into a shot glass and then say, "Look how pretty."

"Booze and strippers are like pasta and sauce.
There never seems to be enough of one to go with the other."

~Dino Tripodis 1994

Pretty Paper. No Pabst Blue Ribbon

Silver and Gold. Two of the colors most associated with Christmas. It's in the tinsel, the gift-wrapping and even in some of the gifts we purchase for our loved ones. It's also a strip club, but that's not important right now.

No big surprise, it's also in my booze, so naturally I had to incorporate it into the holiday mix. Since I was basing the cocktails on their given name, I wanted the ingredients of this drink to actually be from a bottle of silver and a bottle of gold. I know...after eighteen drinks, I'd gone from an imaginative creator of cocktails to a boozy Martha Stewart.

Nevertheless, be honest- if there was a half hour show on everyday where they were making new and exciting cocktails with celebrity guests, you would watch it. I can see it now- GETTIN' CROCKED IN THE COCKTAIL KITCHEN WITH DINO TRIPODIS. Food Network, I await your call.

Day 20 Gramma Got Hung-Over

1 SHOT OF GRAND MARNIER
1 SHOT OF DISARONNO
1/2 CUP OF CRANBERRY JUICE

Mix the shots and the cranberry juice into a shaker with ice and pour into your mom's favorite hi-ball glass. Cap it off with a nice cherry garnish. Serve her enough of them and you won't have to take her to the mall the next day.

"Drink long enough with family and they might eventually start to feel like friends, but never drink so long with friends that they start to feel like family."

~Dino Tripodis 2006

Rela-tipsy

If I remember the conversation with my mother during one particular holiday season, I believe it went something like this.

"Fix me a high ball, Dino. But nothing strong-but not too weak, either. You know- something sweet, but with a little kick to it. I mean, I don't want to get drunk after having just one, so make something I can enjoy a few times throughout the evening. Just make sure I don't "feel it" the next morning. Because tomorrow, I want you to take me to the mall and I don't want a headache before I go somewhere where I know I'm going to get a headache. God, I cannot believe I haven't finished shopping yet. I still have to get something for your sister and you never told me what you wanted this year. Do you need new socks and underwear? Anyway, fix me something nice, but not like that drink you made me last Christmas. Geez, I thought I'd fall off the barstool after one sip. I'm your mother, not one of your poker buddies- and put a little juice in it, too. That would be good. Oh, I know... what was that drink you poured for your grandmother that one year that made her feel so good?"

"A brandy."

"I don't know what's in that, but give me one of those."

Five, Four, Three, Two, DONE!

We were getting close. Five more cocktails to go. Five more days to see a dream come true. Five more days before a true sense of accomplishment would be ours to claim as a victory for not only The Cocktail Coalition, but for drinkers all over the world!

The combinations for drinks were getting harder to create. The commitment to time and tasting was taking its toll on families and relationships. Vocations that had suffered early on in the quest were now in danger of being lost forever in a puddle of mixers and alcohol that none of us had ever seen the likes of before. Well, not really. Aside from myself, everyone in the Cocktail Coalition was self-employed, but drinking every day made us really tired, okay?

As the Coalition nursed their latest drink, I thought to myself- is this what is was like to be close to completing a marathon; trying to find the strength and endurance to close out those last few miles? Is this how Lance Armstrong felt with the finish line in sight at The Tour De France? Is this how it felt to sit through all of The Godfather movies in one day and not give up in the last hour of the truly inferior Godfather Part III?

Runners talk of a certain "high" they achieve at some point, which allows them to break through the barrier of fatigue and pain. To say we had achieved a "drinker's high" seemed a little redundant, but yes- I could see that finish line! I still had names for drinks! I had bottles of liquor that had not yet become a part of The 25 Days of Christmas Cocktailing. And I still had ice. There was no doubt in my mind that I was going to finish this race against the month of December, or throw up trying, dammit!

"Houston, we have NO problem." This mission was going to be completed.

Day 21 **The Bi-Polar Express**

1 1/2 SHOTS OF VODKA
1 SHOT OF EXTRA DRY VERMOUTH
1 SHOT OF CHOCOLATE LIQUER
1 TSP. OF INSTANT EXPRESSO

Put all of the ingredients in a blender with ice and mix for about 20 seconds, or until the ice has been reduced to a frosty smooth state of consumption. The result will end up being a wonderful frozen concoction that's almost as charming as you may think you are.

*"I have far more charm in a tuxedo.
Too bad both have to be back by noon tomorrow."*

~Dino Tripodis 2005

Dressed To The "Nines" And Drunk By Ten

Martini Time. And no bi-polar jokes. It's just a fun play on words, but if I had to choose a personality-altering cocktail, it would be the martini and it would be wrong not to include one in the holiday mix.

Martinis are fun, sophisticated and are consumed in cool-looking glasses. Whenever I have one and I'm not wearing a tuxedo, I feel extremely underdressed. Moreover, when I am wearing a tuxedo, I purposely get a martini because I think its part of the total package. In fact, I think they should include a martini glass when they rent tuxedos.

"Here are your suspenders, your bowtie, and your martini glass because this is what you'll be drinking tonight."

Here is why I love wearing a tuxedo. Nobody looks bad in one. Let me qualify that by saying nobody looks bad in a black one. I'm not including those god-awful, sky blue, lime green, bad beige rentals with the ruffled shirts that you may have worn to prom back in the day. However, the classic black tuxedo can make a chump look like a champ. They exude confidence and cool. Do you think Bond would've looked nearly as smooth ordering a vodka martini in a leisure suit? No. In fact, check out a Roger Moore Bond movie, and you'll get my point. Can you picture The Rat Pack on-stage in Vegas in sport jackets? Absolutely not. Unheard of. And why the formal attire is sometimes referred to as a monkey suit is beyond me, because I think even a monkey looks good in a tuxedo.

"Yes, a vodka martini please, and one for my well-dressed simian friend at the end of the bar."

"The monkey is drinking a gin martini, sir but I'm sure he will appreciate the gesture. He in turn has sent you this banana." That's one class act monkey.

Alcohol in general is sometimes guilty of altering personalities. That being said, tuxedos can accentuate and if necessary even save an altered state of persona.

"Bob was an ass at the benefit last night."

"Yes, he was, but he looked terrific."

So, here's to the drink of formal wear, witty banter, and 5 o'clock-tails all over the world. A little easier on the vermouth next time, if you don't mind.

Day 22 Santa's Slay-Ride

1 SHOT OF VODKA
1 SHOT OF OUZO
1 SPLASH OF CRANBERRY JUICE

Put them all in a shaker with ice, mix and pour into a tall holiday glass, and give the keys to the sleigh to a designated elf.

"Don't get drunk with a Mall Santa.
He doesn't remember anything you asked for."

~Dino Tripodis 2002

Not-So-Secret Santa

Yes, Virginia, there is a Santa Claus and it's your Uncle Frank.

Is there any better example of the early stages of denial than the existence of Santa Claus?

We wanted so much to believe in the Jolly Old Elf as children, we gladly accepted the fact that the guy sitting in a big red velvet chair at the mall making some extra seasonal cash was indeed Santa Claus. Didn't matter that he looked different from year to year, had a fake beard, or sometimes was skinnier than my own mother. He was the guy we needed to see in order to voice aloud what we wanted for Christmas, and if we didn't get what we asked for, our parents were absolved of the disappointment.

Santa took the rap. Santa messed up. Or maybe Santa determined we weren't as good as we said, and the missing present from the wish list was a wake-up call for us to maybe behave a little better the next year.

My favorite moments were the visits from Santa to our house, three or four days before Christmas. Forget for a moment that he looked like one of my father's fat cousins, had liquor on his breath and spoke with a Greek accent. Santa had somehow found time in his busy schedule to stop and ask my sister and me what we personally wanted for Christmas and then afterwards would stay for ouzo and stuffed green peppers.

Of course, nothing lasts forever. I eventually was told there wasn't a real Santa Claus, but my younger sister still believed, so it was an interesting lesson in parenting, watching my mother try to find a nice way to tell her that Santa was too busy to make a personal visit to the house this year. I found out later in life that Santa had apparently gotten a D.U.I. taking his "sleigh" on a test run and wound up doing three days in county lock-up. A year after that, he was convicted on insurance fraud charges and spent the next five Christmases in Joliet Prison making "toys" for the state.

So, this one's for you Santa, along with a "thank you" for the personalized license plate you made me for my BIG WHEEL that one year.

Day 23 **Peach On Earth**

1 SHOT OF PEACH SCHNAPPES
1 SHOT OF BRANDY
1 SHOT OF JAMESONS WHISKEY
SPLASH OF ORANGE JUICE

You can mix this one in a shaker with ice or toss all the
ingredients into a blender. It doesn't matter. This is one
harmonious cocktail and no matter how you put together,
peace will reign.

"Peace On Earth. Goodwill is a great place to buy used golf clubs."

~Dino Tripodis 2007

A Piece Of Mind

Peace On Earth. At least in the city of Columbus, Ohio. You could actually feel the sense of calm as we wrapped up the twenty-third cocktail of the month.

"I can't believe we made it this far. Do you have the last two in mind?" Deli asked.

"Yes, I have names for them and an idea of what they should consist of thematically, but past that, no recipe." I sighed.

"You don't seem too concerned," said Beardman.

"I'm not really. You see my drunken friends, I believe in the true spirit of this season. I always have. Moreover, I don't think that the shaky hand that has guided me thus far would stop with only two cocktails to go. That would not be the Christmas story we'd want to pass on to our future generations. No, I'm not concerned. I have the names for the drinks, and that's enough for now. Trust me. The recipes will come.

"Well, this one is great, and I don't even like peach schnappes," Jamie said.

"I know," I replied. "It's a true Christmas miracle in its own right is it not? To discover an appreciation for liquors that you never once considered before. It's magical, I tell ya, absolutely freakin' magical." I raised a glass.

"Gentlemen, this mission may have started on a lark of an idea, but I think we all know now it's become more than that." I began to choke up with emotion. "It's our calling."

The Cocktail Coalition all nodded in approval as we clinked our glasses and toasted to our premature success, as I never once allowed them to know that I had no idea what the next two cocktails would be.

Day 24 The Night Before Christ-Mess

1⁄2 SHOT OF JACK DANIEL'S
1⁄2 SHOT OF CROWN ROYAL
1⁄2 SHOT OF MAKERS MARK
1⁄2 SHOT OF MYERS DARK RUM
1⁄2 SHOT OF BACARDI GOLD RUM
1⁄2 SHOT OF ABSOLUTE VODKA
1⁄2 SHOT OF TANGERAY GIN
SPLASH OF 7-UP
SPLASH OF CRANBERRY JUICE

If you're an idiot, you can use full shots in this mixture, but I don't advise it. Pour all the shots into a shaker with ice and mix thoroughly. Pour it all into a tall glass and top it off with equal parts of cranberry juice and 7-up. Stir it again to mix it up, then be prepared to "mix-it up."

"The two saddest words in the drinking world are 'last call' only trumped by the four saddest words- 'license and registration, please.'"

~Dino Tripodis 2000

And Drinks On The House

It was Christmas Eve and I wasn't ready. Yes, I had finished my shopping and my presents were wrapped, but I knew at the very least that come Christmas Day, people would be expecting to know what The 25 Days of Christmas Cocktailing consisted of and maybe would even want to try one of them. There was no way I could not produce a finished list. Then it hit me.

"T'was the night before Christmas and all through the house, not a creature was stirring, a good time to get soused."

My apologies to Mr. Moore, but this drink would be the star on my tree, the stuff that made Santa's cheeks red, my Hallelujah Chorus of cocktails! My liquor bottles would become my faithful reindeer as I hitched no less than seven different tastes to this sleigh-full of booze in an attempt to make a concoction that would be a cocktail gift to remember and a Christmas memory that one would struggle to recall the following morning.

To say this drink took its toll on me would be an understatement. I mixed seven different liquors four different times before finding the proper mixture that suited the name I had given it, yet was able to make it taste like a glass of punch at an A.A. meeting.

Do you only have time for one cocktail, but want to feel like you've had seven? Well, then...Merry Christmas. Keys, please.

Day 25 Away In A Manger

1 SHOT OF BLACK SAMBUCA
1 SHOT OF CLEAR SAMBUCA
1 TEA BAG OF BLACK PEKOE TEA
1 LARGE SPOONFUL OF HONEY

Pour the shots into a large mug. Add hot water. Steep the tea bag like you would for any cup of tea, then- "nighty-night."

"When it comes to drinking I've never cared for the term 'over-served'. I prefer to believe that I "under-estimated."

~Dino Tripodis 2009

Sleep In Drunkenly Peace

After twenty-four drinks, a lot of lost time, and a couple bottles of ibuprofen, I felt the title for this last cocktail was appropriate. Away in a Manger is where you should be after an almost month long attempt of celebrating the season.

I wanted the drink to be something soothing, contemplative, and nurturing. A cocktail enjoyed quietly with friends and family as they reminisced over their last twenty-four days of alcohol bliss. A rocking chair cocktail. Something that felt like a cozy blanket on a chilly winter's morn, or a warm towel out of the dryer, or that comforting sense of reckless abandon when you pee in the ocean and nobody is the wiser. Oh, c'mon. You know you've done it. A pool is one thing, but who gets out of an entire ocean to piss? That's when I decided the last cocktail needed to be a tea drink.

"Let me put on some tea." That's what everyone says when they know there's going to be some time spent talking or ruminating over old times. You sip, you think, you sigh, you smile and you sip again. Ah, yes...good times indeed. And, oh look- some butter cookies. Now the table is truly set for a trip down memory lane.

So, enjoy this special blend of potential inebriation, but be wary of a second cup unless of course a long winter's nap is the next thing on your list of "things to do" on Christmas Day. If so, then Merry Cocktailing to all, and to all...good night.

Epilogue

And so the very, merry mission came to an end. It was quite the journey and not without its pitfalls, pratfalls and ponderous moments of doubt. Nevertheless, in the end, a body of work had been created that could very well stand the test of time or at the very least- a last call at your favorite bar or tavern.

There would be no mandatory drinking in what days remained in the month of December. But a favorite cocktail out of the bunch to reflect upon a job well done? Sure. However, when January rolled around, all bets and all cocktails were off the bar. It would be time for a process a comedian friend of mine turned me onto a few years back.

The January Clean Out. No boozing for the entire of month of January. A procedure that allows the body a chance to cleanse itself of the self-inflicted damage it was willingly and at times, unwillingly put through. In addition, it also serves as a sort of drinking litmus test. If for some reason, you cannot make it through the entire month without a cocktail, well then...maybe its time for you to get a different kind of book.

I really don't expect many of you to accomplish all of The 25 Days of Christmas Cocktailing, but instead I ask you to look upon this small tome as a gift and a holiday guide that will keep on giving for many joyous seasons to come. As for me? Well, there are a lot of holidays out there, and the bar is still stocked, so... Anybody up for The 40 Liquors of Lent? I'm kidding. I think.

16743261R00042

Made in the USA
Middletown, DE
20 December 2014